UKULELE

# BLUES

## MASTERY

**UKELIKETHEPROS**

ISBN-13: **978-1-958192-00-9**
**UKELIKETHEPROS.COM**
© 2022 TERRY CARTER

# TABLE OF CONTENTS

# UKULELE
# BLUES
## MASTERY

Welcome to the Ukulele Blues Mastery book by Uke Like The Pros. The Ukulele Blues Mastery book by Terry Carter is the most comprehensive book written for Blues on the ukulele in the universe. Whether you are a beginner at the Blues, or a seasoned veteran, the Ukulele Blues Mastery book is going to take you deep into the world of the Blues, and you will come out a better, more confident ukulele player. The Ukulele Blues Mastery book is going to show you how to play Blues Rhythm, Blues Fingerstyle, Blues Scales, and Blues Soloing for this wonderful four string instrument called the ukulele.

In this book you are going to explore all the techniques and tools that you need to become a Ukulele Blues Master. You are going to learn Blues Shuffle, Blues Rock, Jump Blues, Fingerstyle Blues, Boogie Woogie Blues, Walking Blues, Country Blues, Slow Blues, Jazz Blues, Blues Scales, and Blues Soloing.

You can get the free backing tracks for every lesson in the Ukulele Blues Mastery book at ukelikethepros.com/bluesbook. A complete video course of every lesson (sold separately) is available at **ukelikethepros.com/ukeblues.**

Before we jump into the contents of the Ukulele Blues Mastery book, let's break down the types of ukuleles you can use for this book. Any size, ukulele, soprano, concert, or tenor tuned G-C-E-A will work for this course. Although the Blues sounds best on a ukulele with a Low G string (wound or unwound low G), a ukulele with a High G will work for all these lessons. Although a High G ukulele works, Uke Like The Pros highly suggests either putting on a Low G on your current ukulele or getting another ukulele that has Low G. You can visit the **terrycartermusicstore.com** for any help with either.

The Uke Like The Pros Ukulele Blues Mastery book is a step-by-step introduction to the Blues, which means each lesson will build upon the next, so that you develop the proper techniques and confidence you need to become a Uke Blues Master.

One of the key concepts in this book is understanding Swing and Straight Feel. It's extremely important to not only understand the differences between Swing and Straight, but to be able to flawlessly execute the two styles. Blues Swing is the primary style you hear in the Blues Shuffle, Boogie Woogie, Jazz Blues, Walking Blues, and Slow Blues. Straight Blues is a faster, more driving style that you'll hear in Blues Rock (ala Chuck Berry and Little Richard), Jump Blues, Fingerstyle Blues, and Country Blues. Don't worry if you don't understand this concept right now; you will by the time you are done with the Ukulele Blues Mastery book by Terry Carter.

Although the Ukulele Blues Mastery book will focus on understanding the different styles of Blues rhythms and styles, it does explore other essential topics, such as Fingerstyle Blues, Blues Scales, and the Blues Solo.

The Uke Like The Pros Ukulele Blues Mastery book by Terry Carter is the most comprehensive book on Blues Ukulele in the universe. Make sure to check out additional Blues Ukulele videos in our youtube channel. Are you ready? Let's dive in.

*Get your FREE Backing Tracks for this book:*

# HISTORY OF
# THE BLUES

The Blues has a long history as an American artform dating back to the mid-1800's. The Blues was created out of African Spirituals that were born out of work songs or field songs. These songs were sung not only out of tradition, but to also help pass the time, and became the basis of the Blues that we know today. There are 3 keys parts you want to remember about the Blues:

## 1. Call & Response
This is the where one person or group would sing a phrase and then another person or group would respond to that phrase.

## 2. 12 Bar Blues Form
The 12 Bar Blues is the most common form for all Blues. Although some Blues can be 8 or even 16 bars long, the majority are 12 bars. This is a form you want to get down into your soul, so you know exactly where you are in the form of the 12 Bar Blues at any time.

## 3. Blues Scale
The main scale that is used to create Blues melodies, and to solo, come from the notes of the Blues Scale. The Blues Scale is the same as the Minor Pentatonic Scale except that it has an added "Blue Note" in it (the b5 Note).

---

**a.** For example:
**i. CALL** – "When He Walks In The Joint"     **ii. RESPONSE** – "Everybody Turns To Look"

**b.** Call & Response can also happen between the voice and an instrument. B.B. King is famous for this, as he would sing a phrase (Call) and then answer it with his guitar (Response).

---

The Blues Scale in A would be:
**A – C – D – Eb – E – G – A**

# THE BLUES FORM

The 12 Bar Blues form consists of 12 bars (or measures) that repeat over and over again and alternate between the I, IV, and V chords (usually seventh chords). If you are in the key of A, it would be called Blues in A, the I chord would be A7, the IV chord would be D7, and the V chord would be E7.

In a 12 Bar Blues in A, bars 1-4 are played on the A7 chord, bars 5-6 on the D7, bars 7-8 return to the A7, bar 9 on the E7, and bar 10 on the D7. The last 2 bars (11-12) are called The Turnaround. Bar 11 returns to the A7 and bar 12 goes back to the E7 before it repeats.

12 Bar Blues in A

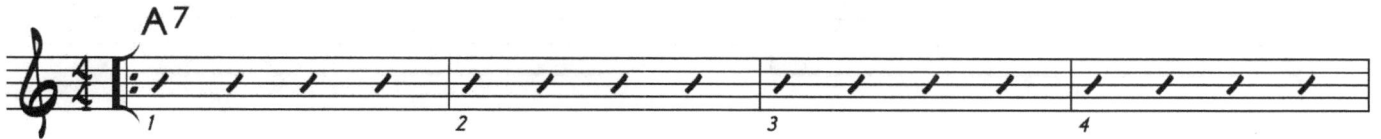

# UNDERSTANDING SWING 1/8th NOTES

As a Blues Master it is absolutely necessary to be able to switch between playing Swing 1/8th notes and Straight 1/8 notes. Straight 1/8th notes are the easiest because all you have to do is divide the quarter note beat into 2 equal parts and count them 1 + 2 + 3 + 4 +. You'll hear Straight 1/8th notes in Blues Rock, Country Blues, and Jump Blues.

## STRAIGHT 1/8th NOTES

Swing 1/8th notes are a little harder to play and many times you'll hear people say, "just feel it." Although playing swing 1/8th notes is a feeling, you must understand how to divide the beat and play them properly. Let's start with a triplet, which is 3 notes per beat, and counted 1-trip-let, 2 trip-let, 3 trip-let, 4 trip-let.

## TRIPLETS

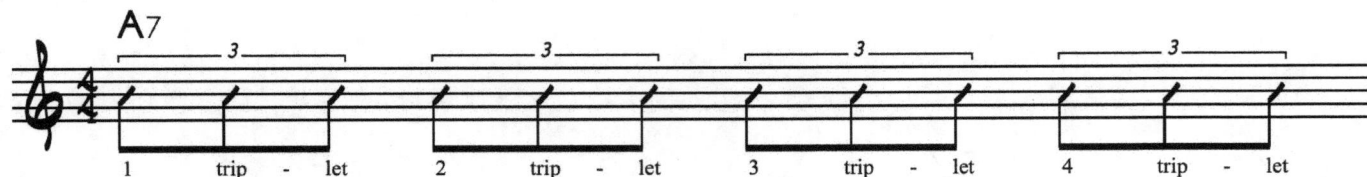

Now that you have mastered the triplets, to play Swing 1/8th notes simply play the first and the third note of each triplet, or don't play the middle note of the triplet "trip."ww

## SWING 1/8th NOTES

You'll hear Swing 1/8th notes in Blues Shuffle, Boogie Woogie, Jazz Blues, and Slow Blues.

# STRAIGHT VS SWING 1/8th NOTES

In this lesson you will work on switching between straight and swing 1/8th notes. Use the E chord to play straight 1/8th notes for bars 1-2 and then switch to swing 1/8th notes for bars 3-4 and then repeat. It helps to play this with the backing track which will guide you through the straight and swing 1/8th nots. Get the backing tracks at ukelikethepros.com/bluesbook

Swing vs. Straight

♩=100

Counting:  1  +  2  +  3  +  4  +

Straight 1/8 Notes

4 Times

1  trip - let  2  trip - let  3  trip - let  4  trip - let

Swing 1/8 Notes

# STRUMMING BLUES IN A

This lesson will be a traditional 12 Bar Blues form in "A" played with Swing 1/8th notes. This strum pattern will be a core rhythm that you can play over many types of Blues. The rhythm will be all Swing 1/8th notes with a tie going from the "+ of 2" to beat "3". This means that you strum all the beats using a down-up pattern, but you will not strum beat 3 because of the tie. The only chords you need for this Strumming Blues is A7, D7, and E7.

# STRUMMING BLUES IN A *WITH QUICK-CHANGE*

Are you ready to be blown away? In this lesson you will learn the quick-change. A quick-change is simple and extremely vital as a Blues player. This lesson uses the same rhythm as the previous lesson, but uses a quick-change and a muted strum on beats "2" and 4". A quick-change is when you go to the IV (D7) chord in measure two. The 1st four measures will be A7 – D7 – A7 – A7. The muted strum is indicated by "x." This mute is done with the palm of your strumming hand and can be referred to as palm muting or "chucking." To get the mute, the side of your strumming palm is going to lightly touch all the strings an instant before you strum.

# WALKING THE BLUES IN A

Up to this point you have been working on strumming, but let's play a Blues with all single notes. In this Walking The Blues lesson, you will play a cool single note pattern that will not only sound cool but be a great technique builder. You can play this lesson using your thumb and use the fingerings indicated.

Shuffle Walking Blues

♩=96

**A**

Fingering:  2  2  1  1  2  2  3  4  *Sim...*

TAB: 2—2 1—1—2—2—3—4

**D7**

1  1  1  1  2  2  3  4

TAB: 2—2 2—2—3—3—4—5

**A**

2  2  1  1  2  2  3  4

TAB: 2—2 1—1—2—2—3—4

**E7**   **D7**   **A**   **E7**   **A**

1 1 1 1 2 2 3 4   1 1 1 1 2 2 3 4   2 2 1 1 2 2 3 3   4 4 2 2 1 1 4 4   2

TAB:
E7: 4—4 4—4—5—5—6—7
D7: 2—2 2—2—3—3—4—5
A: 2—2 1—1—2—2—3—3
E7: 4—4—2—2—1—1
A: 4—4 2

# A7 ◁ SCHOOL

Private Virtual & In-Person Lessons.
All Instruments.

# BOOGIE WOOGIE IN A *OPEN CHORDS*

This lesson will take what you learned in the Strumming Blues but take it up a level by adding some moving melody notes to each open chord. By simply adding these moving melody notes on beats "2" and "4", you create a style called Boogie Woogie. This Boogie Woogie sound is something that was taken from piano players and adapts very well to Ukulele Blues.

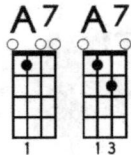
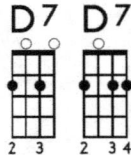
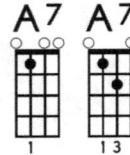

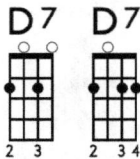
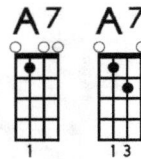

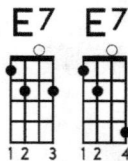
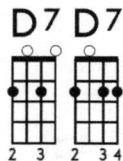
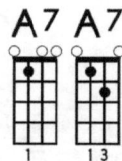
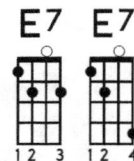

# BOOGIE WOOGIE IN A *POWER CHORDS*

Now it's time to step up your Blues playing. We are still going to be in the key of A and playing the Boogie Woogie, but instead of open position chords, we are going to use 2-string power chords. All these are closed power chords because they do not use any open strings. The A chord will stretch your fingers a bit and require more strength. Also notice the coolest Blues Turnaround ever in measures 11-12, using single note triplets. Triplets are when you play 3 notes in one beat.

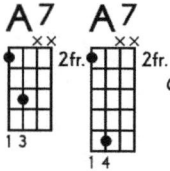
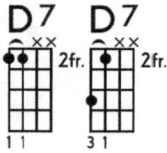
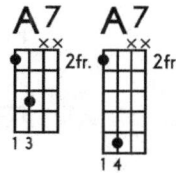

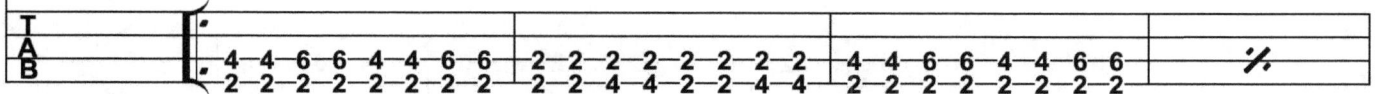

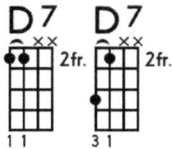
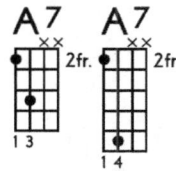

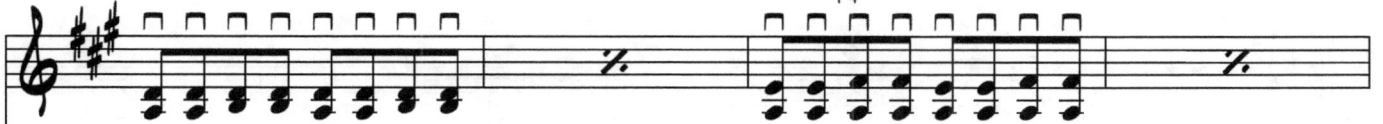

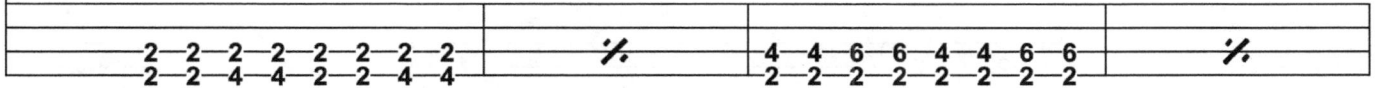

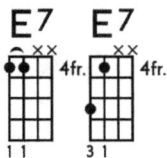
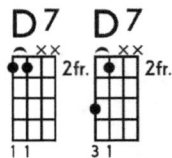

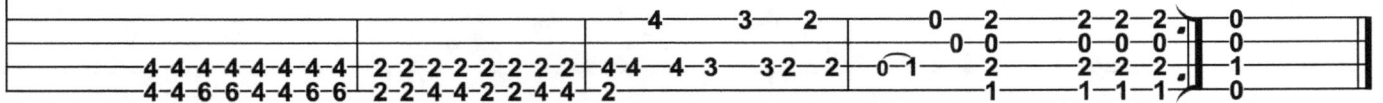

12

# FINGERSTYLE BLUES IN A

This will be a Blues in A with a twist. The twist is that we are going to play this piece fingerstyle with straight 1/8th notes and has a hip turnaround. The fingerstyle pattern is a one bar pattern that is going to use all four fingers of your picking hand: p (thumb), i (index), m (middle), and a (ring) fingers. Although this pattern may take you a bit to master, it is a pattern that really works for any song with a Country/Americana vibe to it. The hip turnaround is A7 – D7 – A7 – E7 with each chord getting "2" beats. Once you get the finger picking pattern down, you can apply it to your favorite song.

# BLUES ROCK IN A

Chuck Berry style anyone? Did you know that the early Rock and Roll stars, such as Chuck Berry, Elvis, Little Richard, Buddy Holly, and Jerry Lewis took the slower Blues Shuffle and sped it up, played straight 1/8th notes, and added fun lyrics about cars, love, and partying to create Rock and Roll? It's true. Even though Rock and Roll borrowed from R & B (Rhythm & Blues), Country, and Pop music in the 1950's, it took the most from Rhythm & Blues. This piece is in the key of A and will go back to the open position power chords, but by playing straight 1/8th notes and changing the Boogie Woogie pattern to a faster driving rock feel.

# JUMP BLUES IN A

For this Jump Blues you are going to continue playing straight 1/8th notes, but it will weave between single notes and chord strums. The single notes are a 2-bar walking bass pattern that can be played with your thumb. In the next 2 bars you will play a strum pattern with mutes using your index finger. The last 4 bars use all single notes and has a 1st and 2nd ending (play the 1st ending the 1st time and after you repeat skip the 1st ending and play the 2nd ending). The piece ends with the climatic A7#9 chord which is also referred to as the Jimi Hendrix chord.

# COUNTRY BLUES IN A

If Johnny Cash were with us today, he would dig a strum pattern like this. This is known as the Bass Strum pattern, because on beats "1" and "3" you play a bass note, and on beats "2" and "4" you use a down-up strum pattern. Notice the bass notes alternate between the 4th and the 3rd string on beats "1" and "3." The challenge is keeping the beat steady and hitting the right bass notes of each chord.

Johnny Cash Country Blues

♩=120

Counting: 1 + 2 + 3 + 4 + *Sim...*

# SLOW 12/8 FEEL BLUES IN A

The Slow 12/8 Blues is one of the coolest styles that you can play. Although it's written in 4/4 time it has a 12/8 feel due to the triplets (3 notes per beat) throughout the piece. This Blues has a jazzy sound adding more than just the I, IV, and V chords you normally see in a Blues. The things you'll notice are the addition of ½ step slides (A7 to Bb7 and E7 to F7) walk ups (A7 – Bmin7 – C#min7 – Cmin7), Minor 7th chords, and the E7+ chord (aka E7 augmented or #5 chord). Take your time with this one and make sure to get these chords in your hands and ear. This Blues feel can be heard in the style of songs such as Stormy Monday by T-Bone Walker and The Allman Brothers.

# SLOW 12/8 FEEL BLUES IN A

*PG. 2 of 2*

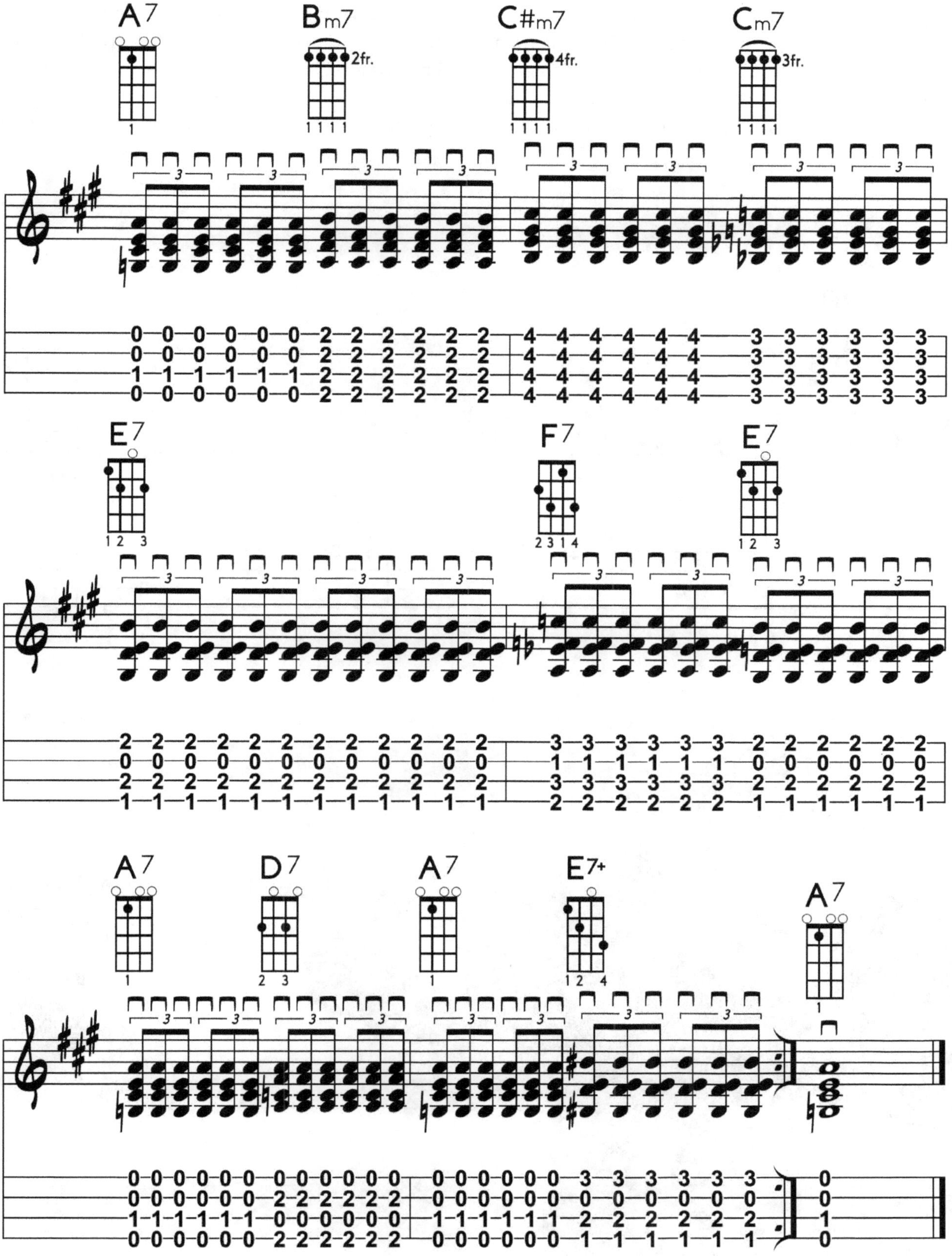

# BLUES SCALE IN A

The Blues Scale is the most widely used and important scales used in the Blues, as it forms the foundation for Blues melodies and soloing. The Minor Pentatonic is another important scale, but if you can play the Blues Scale, you can play the Minor Pentatonic Scale since the Blues Scale only adds one additional note, the flat 5 (b5). The notes of the Blues Scale in A are A – C – D – Eb – E – G. For this lesson you will learn a 1-½ octave Blues Scale in A that starts on the note (4th string – 2nd fret) and goes up to the E note (1st string – 7th fret). Make sure to memorize this scale to get it i your fingers and ear. Master playing the scale ascending (from 4th to 1st string) before tackling the descending part

# WHAT THE STUDENTS SAY:

I'm pretty new to the ukulele and am so happy that I stumbled upon your website. I've learned more in the last week of being a Premium Member, than in the last few months of trying to figure it out on my own by watching Youtube! I'm really enjoying your easy approach and teaching style. Thank you Terry. I appreciate that you are making yourself accessible for all us newbies with such rudimentary questions. And again, thank

you for offering such great, detailed, easy to follow courses that even a no previous musical knowledge total beginner like me can understand and follow.

## Linda Jones
UKULELE STUDENT.

# BLUES SOLO IN A
*PG. 1 of 2*

It's time to put everything together and learn your first solo. This solo uses a combination of the strum patterns you have been working on and licks from the Blues Scale. Licks are short musical phrases that are taken from the scale. To make the solo sound more authentic, you will be playing Bends (where you bend a note up to a higher pitch) and Hammer On's (play a note and then "hammer" your finger onto another note without picking that note). One of the challenges you will face in this piece is switching from the strumming to the single notes.

# BLUES SOLO IN A

*PG. 2 of 2*

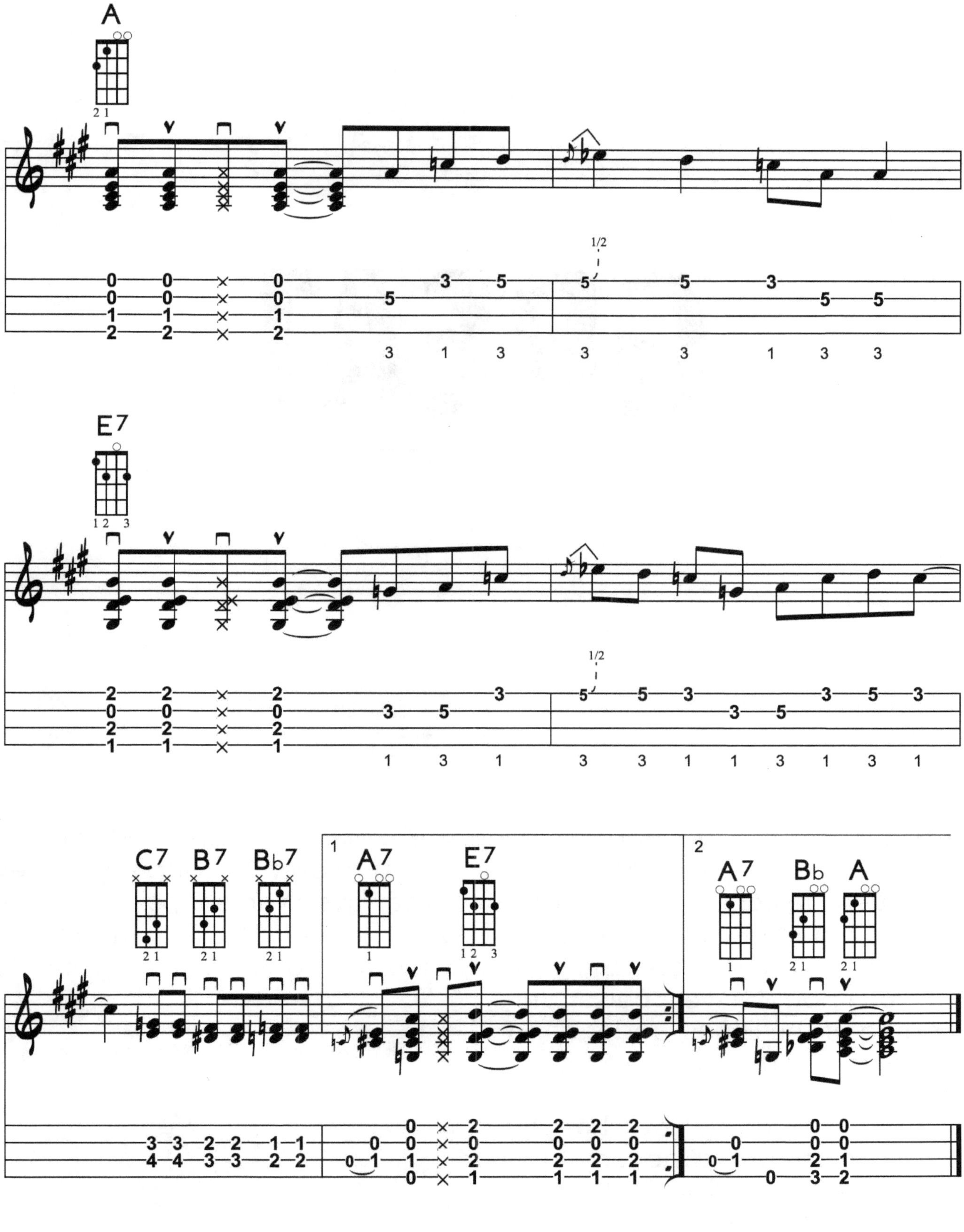

# GREAT
## JOB!

I want to congratulate you for getting through the Uke Like The Pros Ukulele Blues Mastery book by Terry Carter. I am proud of you for making the commitment to yourself and your playing. You should have a better understanding of the Blues, understand Swing vs Straight rhythm, be a better ukulele player, play with better time, and be more confident. Now that you are a Blues Master it is time for you to take the next step in your playing by signing up to our FREE Platinum Membership. Platinum Members have access to over 25 Courses, Challenges, Giveaways, Workshops, and LIVE Q&A with the entire ULTP Nation.
You owe it to yourself and your playing

Get your FREE Membership:

# THE ESSENTIALS

It is important to learn and memorize these terms and symbols because they not only apply to ukulele but to all music.

Treble Clef or "G" Clef

Staff

Time Signature

Measure Numbers

Measure or Bar

Bar Line

End

Top Number:
How Many Beats Per Measure

♩= 120 — Tempo Marks
120 bpm (beats per minute)

Bottom Number:
What Kind of Note Gets the Beat

Common Time:
Same as 4/4 Time

Repeat Sign

**Notes On The Staff:** There are seven notes in music (A, B, C, D, E, F, G) and they move up and down alphabetically on the staff.

G A B C D E F G A B C D E F G A B C D E F

**How To Remember The Notes:**

Notes On The Lines

Notes in The Spaces

E (every)   G (good)   B (boy)   D (does)   F (fine)      F   A   C   E

# HOW TO READ TAB

Tablature (TAB) is a form of music reading for ukulele that uses a 4 line staff and numbers. Each line of the staff represents a string on the ukulele and the numbers represent which fret you play on. When looking at the TAB staff it reads like it's upside down on the paper compared to the strings of your ukulele. On the TAB staff, the highest line (closest to the sky) represents the 1st string (A string) of the ukulele, while the lowest line (closest to the ground) represents the 4th string (G string) of the ukulele. When you see 2 or more notes stacked on top of each other on the TAB staff, that means you play those notes at the same time, like a a chord.

## UKULELE STRINGS

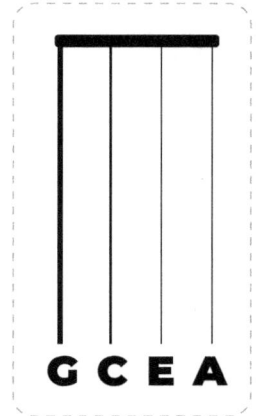

## 1rst STRING EXAMPLES

1) A string. FIRST FRET.
2) A string. THIRD FRET.
3) A string. FIFTH FRET.

**2nd STRING -** E string. THIRD FRET.

**3rd STRING -** C string. SECOND FRET.

**4th STRING -** G string. SIXTH FRET.

**CHORD** C

**ARPEGGIO**
USING THE C CHORD

**PINCH**
USING THE C CHORD

# NOTES ON THE UKULELE NECK

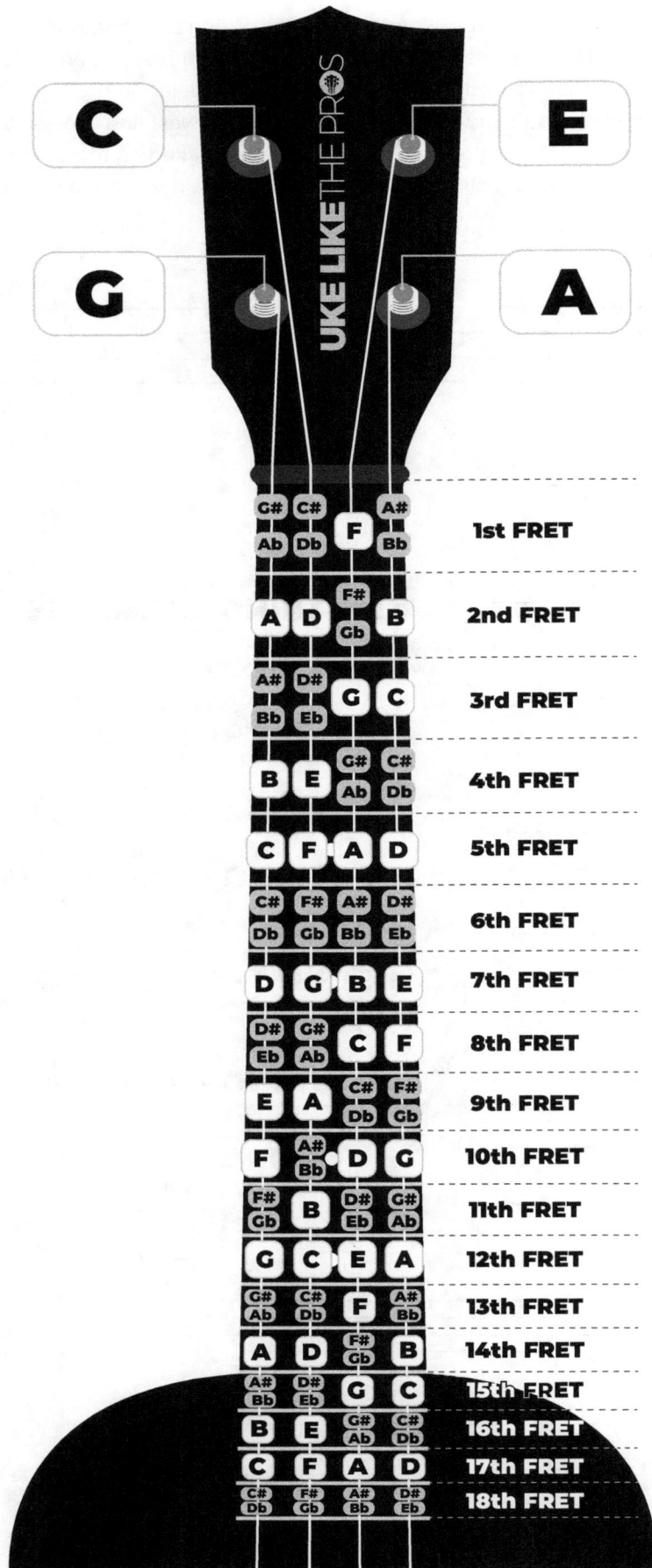

C     E

UKE LIKE THE PROS

G     A

| String 1 | String 2 | String 3 | String 4 | Fret |
|----------|----------|----------|----------|------|
| G#/Ab | C#/Db | F | A#/Bb | 1st FRET |
| A | D | F#/Gb | B | 2nd FRET |
| A#/Bb | D#/Eb | G | C | 3rd FRET |
| B | E | G#/Ab | C#/Db | 4th FRET |
| C | F | A | D | 5th FRET |
| C#/Db | F#/Gb | A#/Bb | D#/Eb | 6th FRET |
| D | G | B | E | 7th FRET |
| D#/Eb | G#/Ab | C | F | 8th FRET |
| E | A | C#/Db | F#/Gb | 9th FRET |
| F | A#/Bb | D | G | 10th FRET |
| F#/Gb | B | D#/Eb | G#/Ab | 11th FRET |
| G | C | E | A | 12th FRET |
| G#/Ab | C#/Db | F | A#/Bb | 13th FRET |
| A | D | F#/Gb | B | 14th FRET |
| A#/Bb | D#/Eb | G | C | 15th FRET |
| B | E | G#/Ab | C#/Db | 16th FRET |
| C | F | A | D | 17th FRET |
| C#/Db | F#/Gb | A#/Bb | D#/Eb | 18th FRET |

C

# UKULELE HANDS

When playing fingerstyle on your ukulele, you will see both letters and numbers to indicate which fingers to use both for picking hand and your fretting hand. These letters and numbers will show up in the music notation, TAB, and chord diagrams.

| FRETTING HAND | PICKING HAND |
|---|---|
| The left hand for right-handed players. will be indicated in the music or chord diagrams by numbers:<br><br>**1**=Index finger  **3**=Ring finger<br>**2**=Middle finger  **4**=Pinky finger | The right hand for right-handed players. will be indicated in the music by letters:<br><br>**p**=Thumb  **m**= Middle<br>**i**= Index  **a**= Ring  **c**=Pinky (not used in this course) |

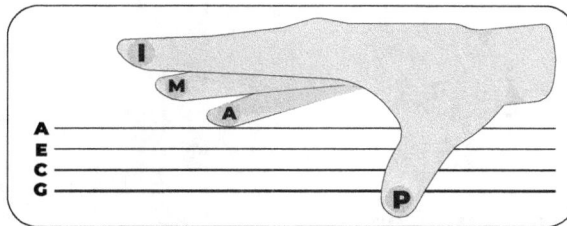

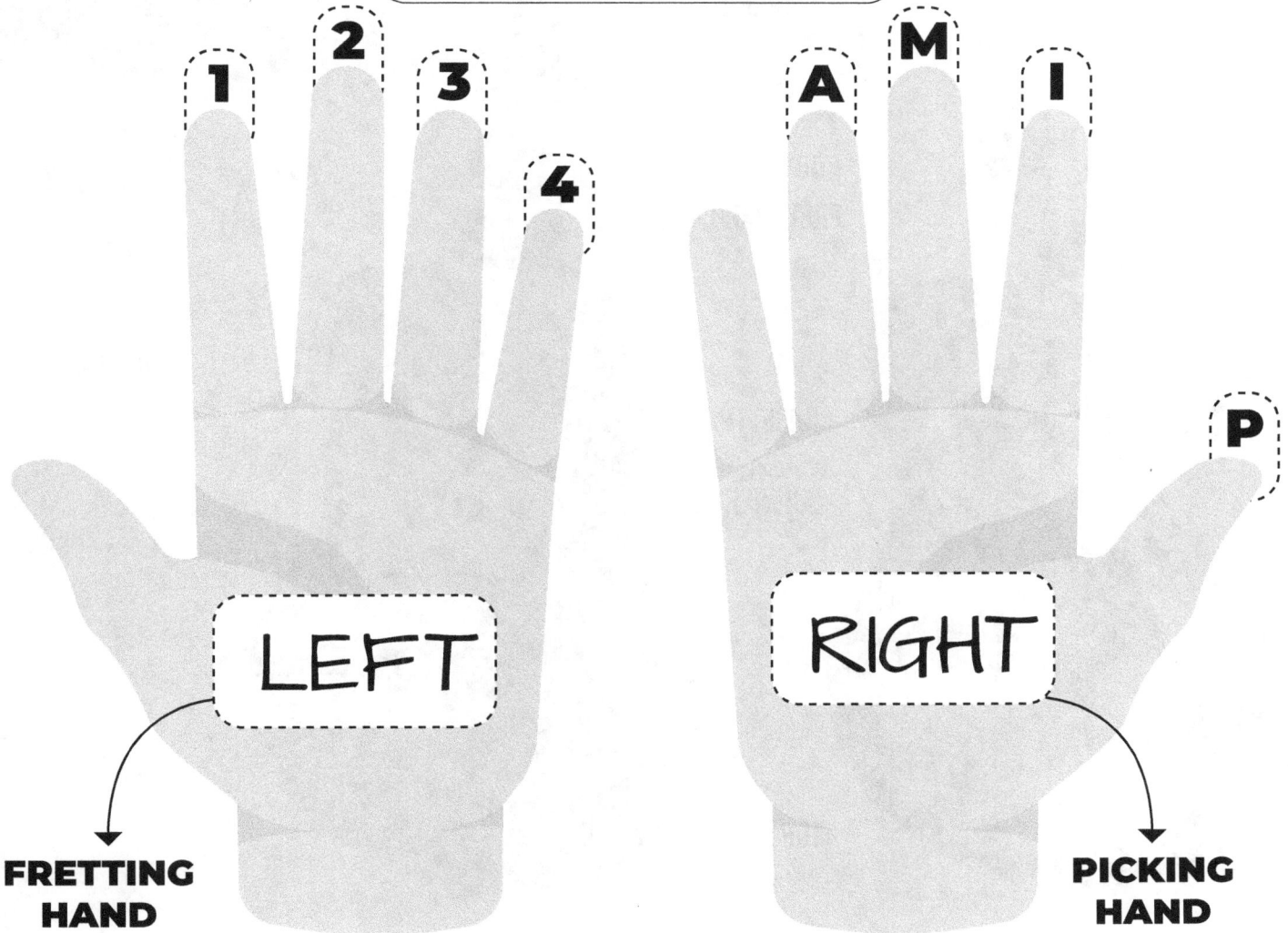

LEFT

RIGHT

**FRETTING HAND**

**PICKING HAND**

# UKULELE PARTS

HEADSTOCK

ULTP SIGNATURE

STRINGS

NUT

FRETS

FRET MARKERS
ON FRETBOARD

SIDE DOTS

SIDE

BODY
FRETBOARD

ROSETTE

SOUND HOLE

TOP

BRIDGE

TUNERS

SADDLE

NECK

BUTT

HEEL

BINDING

SIDE

BACK

# UNDERSTANDING CHORD DIAGRAMS

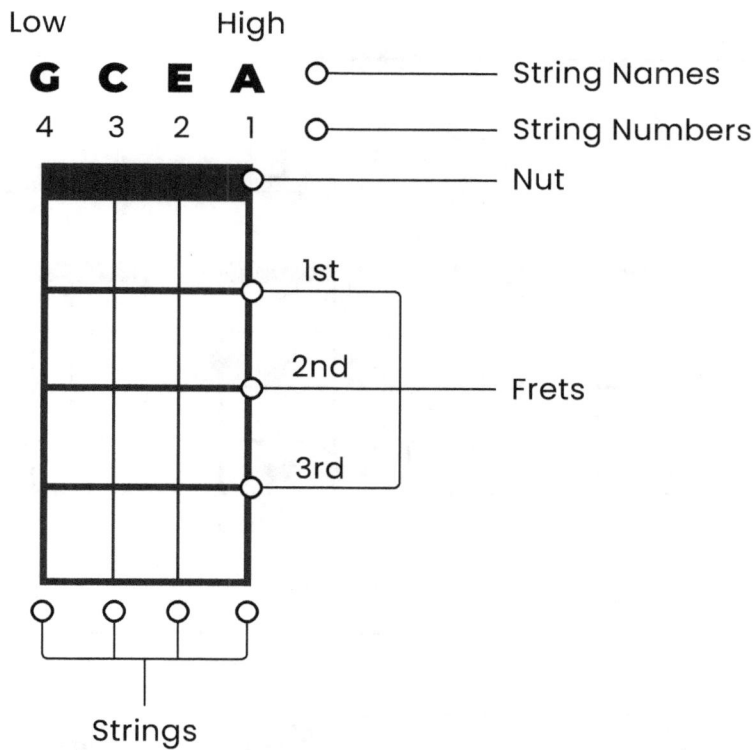

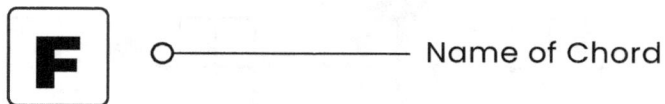

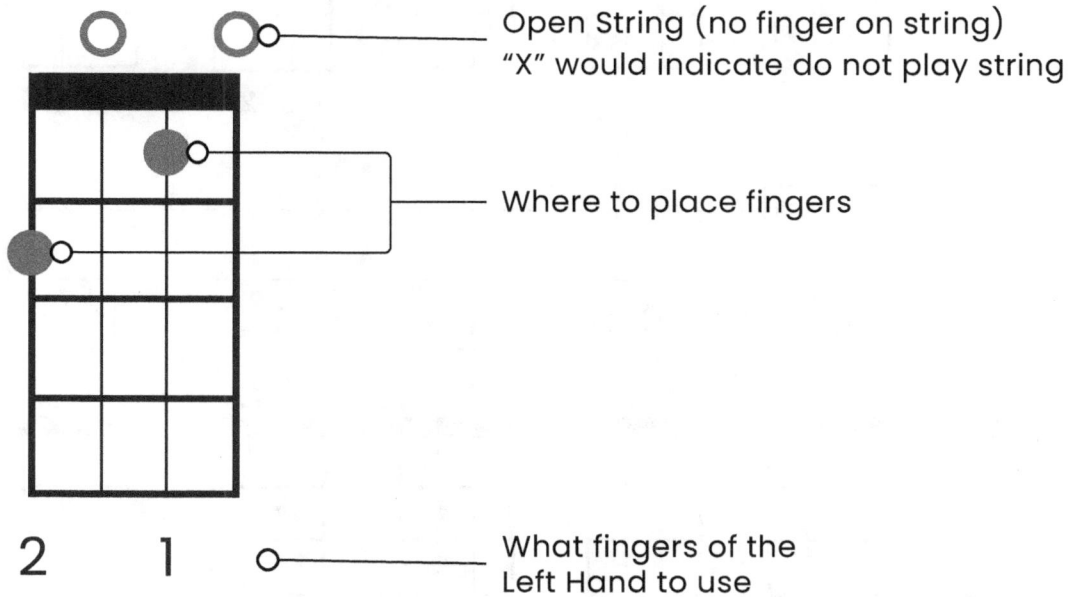

Low          High

**G   C   E   A**  ○———————— String Names

4   3   2   1  ○———————— String Numbers

○———————— Nut

1st

2nd  ——— Frets

3rd

Strings

**F**  ○———————— Name of Chord

○  ○○———— Open String (no finger on string)
"X" would indicate do not play string

———— Where to place fingers

2     1  ○———————— What fingers of the
Left Hand to use

F

# CHORD CHART

These are some of the most widely used chords in all of music. Although there are more chords that are listed, these chords represent the most widely used shapes.

## MAJOR CHORDS

| A | B | C | D | E | F | G |
|---|---|---|---|---|---|---|
| 2 1 | 3 2 1 1 | 3 | 1 1 2 | 2 2 3 1 | 2 1 | 1 3 2 |

## MINOR CHORDS

| A min | B min | C min | D min | E min | F min | G min |
|---|---|---|---|---|---|---|
| 2 | 3 1 1 1 | 3 1 1 1 | 2 3 1 | 3 2 1 | 3 4 2 1 | 2 3 1 |

B min: 2nd FRET
C min: 3rd FRET
E min: 2nd FRET
F min: 3rd FRET

## DOMINANT 7th CHORDS

| A⁷ | B⁷ | C⁷ | D⁷ | E⁷ | F⁷ | G⁷ |
|---|---|---|---|---|---|---|
| 1 | 3 2 1 | 1 | 2 3 | 1 2 3 | 2 3 1 4 | 2 1 3 |

## MAJOR 7th CHORDS

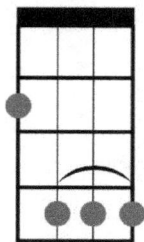
**A** maj⁷

1 3 3 3

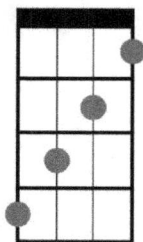
**B** maj⁷

4 3 2 1

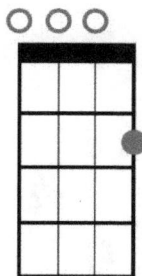
**C** maj⁷

2

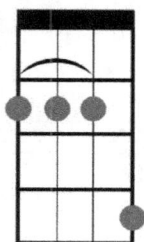
**D** maj⁷

1 1 1 3

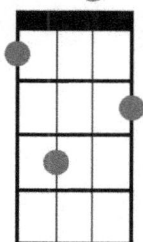
**E** maj⁷

1 3 2

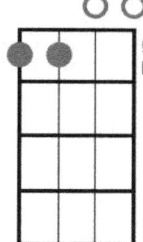
**F** maj⁷

2 3

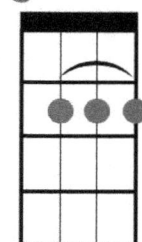
**G** maj⁷

1 1 1

## MINOR 7th CHORDS

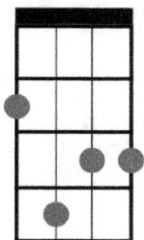
**A** min⁷

1 4 2 3

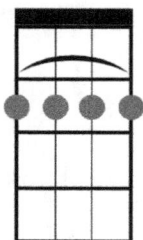
**B** min⁷

1 1 1 1

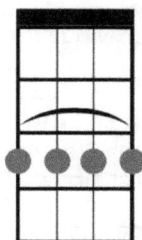
**C** min⁷

1 1 1 1

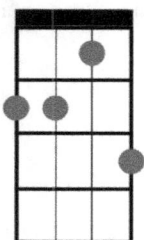
**D** min⁷

2 3 1 4

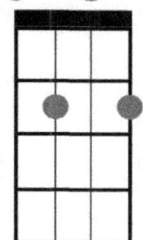
**E** min⁷

2 3

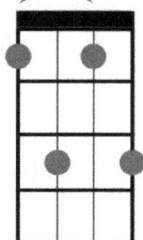
**F** min⁷

1 3 1 4

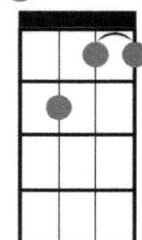
**G** min⁷

2 1 1

## SUS + ADD CHORDS

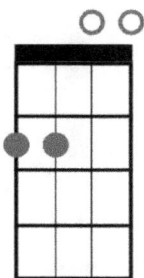
**A** sus⁴

2 3

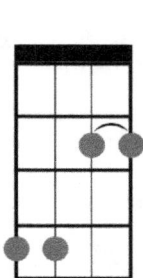
**B** sus⁴

3 4 1 1

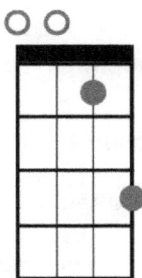
**C** sus⁴

1 3

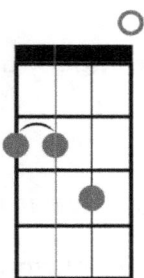
**D** sus⁴

1 1 3

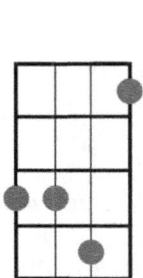
**E** sus⁴

2 3 4 1

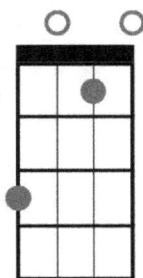
**F** add⁴

3 1

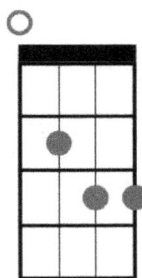
**G** sus⁴

1 3 4

**H**

# MUSIC SYMBOLS TO KNOW

A variety of symbols, articulations, repeats, hammer on's, pull off's, bends, and slides.

**Fermata:**
Hold note

**Staccato:**
Play note short

**Accent:**
Play note loud

**Accented Staccato:**
Play note
loud + short

**Vibrato**
Rapid "shaking"
of note

**Arpeggiated Chord:**
Play the notes in fast
succession from low
to high strings

**Grace Note:**
Fast embellishment
note played before
the main note

**Mute:**
"Muffle" sound of
strings either with
left or right hand

**Down Stroke:**
Pick string(s) with a
downward motion

**Up Stroke:**
Pick string(s) with
an upward motion

**Tie:**
Play first note but
do not play second
note that it is tied to

**Ledger Lines:**
Extend the staff
higher or lower.

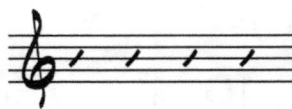

**Slash Notation:**
Repeat notes & rhythms
from previous measure

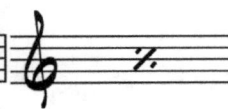

**1 Bar Repeat:**
Repeat notes &
rhythms from
previous measure

**2 Bar Repeat:**
Repeat notes & rhythms
from previous 2 measures

**Repeat Sign:**
(Beginning)

**Repeat Sign:**
(End)

**1st Ending:**
Play this part the
first time only

**2nd Ending:**
Play this part
the second time

**(D.C. AL FINE)** — *D.C.* (da capo) means go to the beginning of the tune and stop when you get to *Fine*

**(D.C. AL CODA)** — *D.C.* means go to the beginning of the tune and jump to *Coda* ⊕ when you see the sign ⊕

**(D.S. AL FINE)** — *D.S.* (dal segno) means go to the *Sign* 𝄋 and stop when you get to *Fine*

**(D.S. AL CODA)** — *D.S.* means go to the *Sign* 𝄋 And Jump to the *Coda* ⊕ when you see ⊕

*SIM...* — Play the same rhythm, strum pattern, or picking pattern as the previous measure

*ETC...* — Continue the same rhythm, strum pattern, or picking pattern as the previous measure

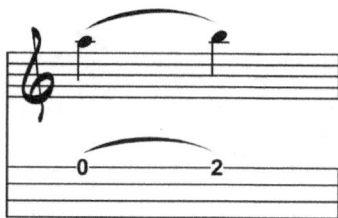

**Hammer On:**
Pick first note then hammer on to the next note without picking it.

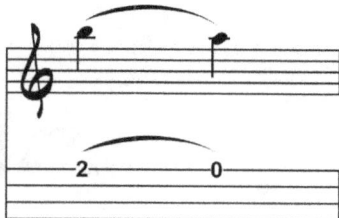

**Pull Off:**
Pick first note then pull off to the next note without picking it.

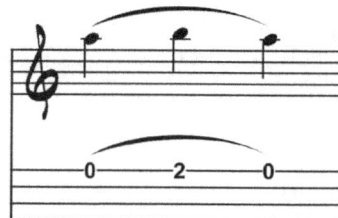

**Hammer On & Pull Off:**
Pick first note, hammer on to the next note, and pull off to the last note all in one motion.

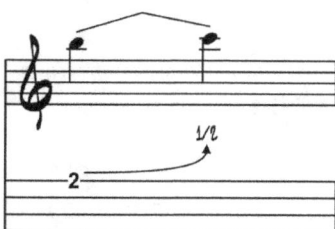

**1/2 Step Bend:**
Bend the first note a 1/2 step or 1 fret.

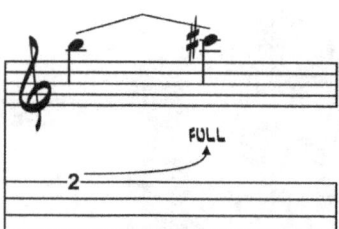

**Whole Step Bend:**
Bend the first note a whole step or 2 frets.

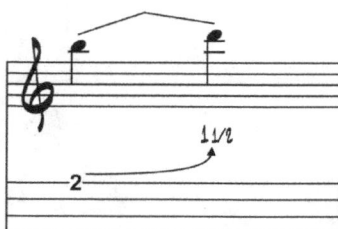

**Step & 1/2 Bend:**
Bend the first note 1 1/2 steps or 3 frets.

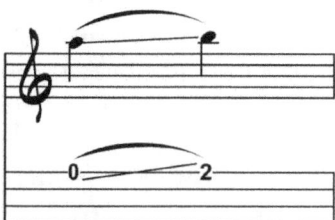

**Forward Slide:**
Pick first note and slide up to higher note.

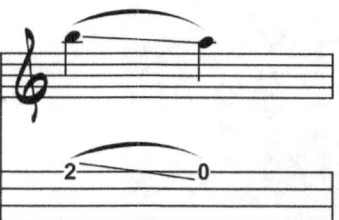

**Backward Slide:**
Pick first note and slide back to lower note.

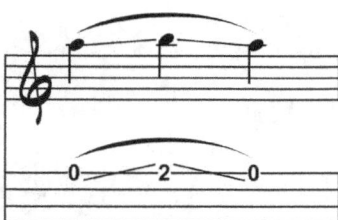

**Forward/Backward Slide:**
Pick first note, slide up to next note and then slide back.

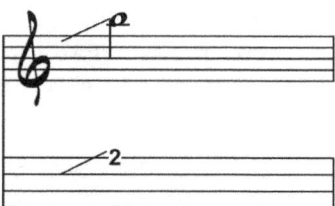

**Slide Into Note:**
Slide from 2-3 frets below note.

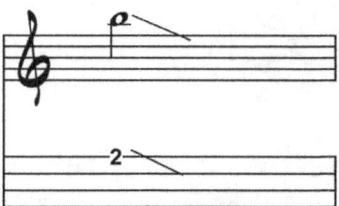

**Slide Off Note:**
Slide off 2-5 frets after note.

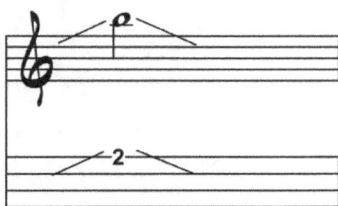

**Slide Into Note then Slide Off Note.**

# ABOUT THE AUTHOR

## TERRY CARTER

Terry Carter is a San Diego-based ukulele player, surfer, songwriter, and creator of ukelikethepros.com, rock-likethepros.com and terrycartermusicstore.com.

With over 25 years as a professional musician, educator and Los Angeles studio musician, Terry has worked with greats like Weezer, Josh Groban, Robby Krieger (The Doors), 2-time Grammy winning composer Christopher Tin (Calling All Dawns), Duff McKagan (Guns N' Roses), Grammy winning producer Charles Goodan (Santana/ Rolling Stones), and the Los Angeles Philharmonic. Terry has written and produced tracks for commercials (Discount Tire and Puma) and TV shows, including Scorpion (CBS), Pit Bulls & Parolees (Animal Planet), Trippin', Wildboyz, and The Real World (MTV). He has self-published over 10 books for Uke Like The Pros and Rock Like The Pros, filmed over 30 ukulele and guitar online courses, and has over 150,000 subscribers on his Uke Like The Pros YouTube channel.

Terry received a Master of Music in Studio/Jazz Guitar Performance from University of Southern California and a Bachelor of Music from San Diego State University, with an emphasis in Jazz Studies and Music Education. He has taught at the University of Southern California, San Diego State University, Santa Monica College, Miracosta College, and Los Angeles Trade Tech College.

K

# ONLINE UKULELE COURSES

The perfect place to learn how to play Ukulele, Baritone Ukulele, Guitar and Guitarlele.

## ULTP Roadmap
## WHERE TO START?

**1) UKULELE BEGINNER**
A.   Beginning Ukulele Starter Course
B.   Beginning Ukulele Bootcamp Course
C.   Ukulele Fundamentals Course
D.   Ukulele Practice & Technique Course
E.   Master the Ukulele 1

**2) UKULELE INTERMEDIATE**
A.   Master The Ukulele 2
B.   Beginning Music Reading
C.   23 Ultimate Chord Progressions
D.   Beginning Ukulele Fingerstyle Course

**3) UKULELE ADVANCED**
A.   Ukulele Blues Mastery Course
B.   Beginning Ukulele Soloing Course
C.   Fingerstyle Mastery Course
D.   Jazz Swing Mastery Course

### MORE OPTIONS!

**FUNLAND**
A.   Beginning Ukulele Kids Course Songbook
B.   21 Popular Songs for Ukulele
C.   The Best Ukulele Christmas Songs
D.   10 Classic Rock Licks
E.   Guitar Fundamentals

**BARITONE UKULELE**
A.   Beginning Baritone Ukulele Bootcamp Course
B.   6 Weeks Baritone Q&A
C.   Baritone Blues Mastery Course
D.   Beginning Baritone Fingerstyle Course

**GUITARLELE**
A.   Guitarlele Starter Course
B.   6 Weeks Guitarlele Q&A
C.   Guitarlele Course for Ukulele and Guitar Players
D.   Guitarlele Blues Mastery Course

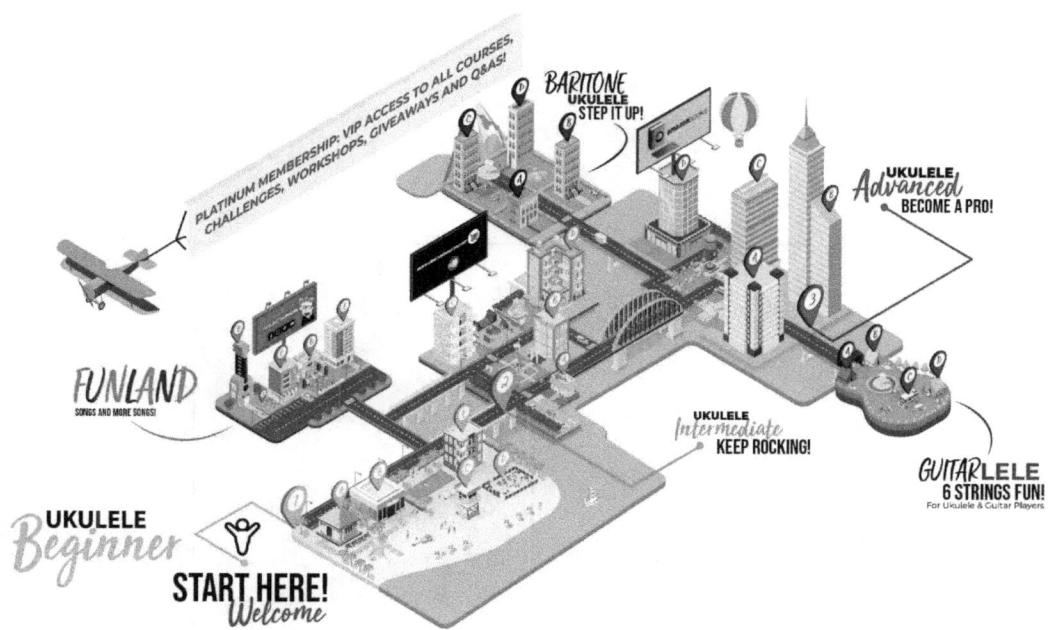

PLATINUM MEMBERSHIP: VIP ACCESS TO ALL COURSES, CHALLENGES, WORKSHOPS, GIVEAWAYS AND Q&AS!

**BARITONE UKULELE** STEP IT UP!

**UKULELE** *Advanced* BECOME A PRO!

**FUNLAND** SONGS AND MORE SONGS!

**UKULELE** *Intermediate* KEEP ROCKING!

**GUITARLELE** 6 STRINGS FUN! For Ukulele & Guitar Players

**UKULELE** *Beginner*

## START HERE! *Welcome*

GUITARLELE BLUES MASTERY COURSE

UKULELE MUSIC READING COURSE

23 ULTIMATE CHORD PROGRESSIONS COURSE

GUITARLELE FOR UKULELE & GUITAR PLAYERS COURSE

BEGINNING UKULELE SOLOING COURSE

CHRISTMAS SONGS FOR UKULELE COURSE

BEGINNING UKULELE BOOTCAMP COURSE

BEGINNING BARITONE UKULELE BOOTCAMP

BEGINNING UKULELE STARTER COURSE

21 POPULAR SONGS FOR UKULELE

BEGINNING BARITONE FINGERSTYLE COURSE

INTERMEDIATE MASTER THE UKULELE #2 COURSE

BEGINNING PRACTICE & TECHNIQUE BOOTCAMP

UKULELE FINGERSTYLE COURSE

BEGINNING UKULELE FINGERSTYLE COURSE

UKULELE BLUES MASTERY COURSE

BARITONE BLUES MASTERY COURSE

BEGINNING MASTER THE UKULELE #1 COURSE

JAZZ SWING MASTERY #1 COURSE

KIDS UKULELE COURSE

## Courses For All Levels
## UKELIKETHEPROS.COM

# TERRY CARTER MUSIC STORE

All your music needs at the #1 music store, **terrycartermusicstore.com**

Baritones

Ukuleles

Guitars

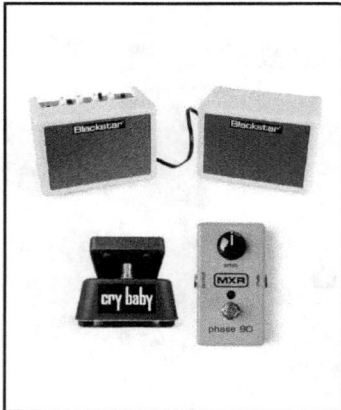

Amplifiers and Pedals

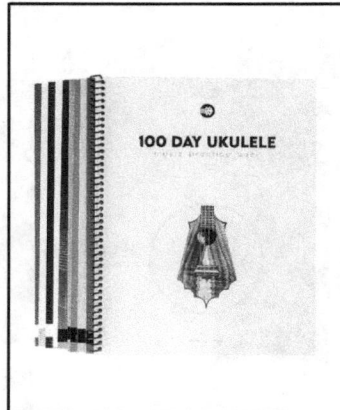

Books

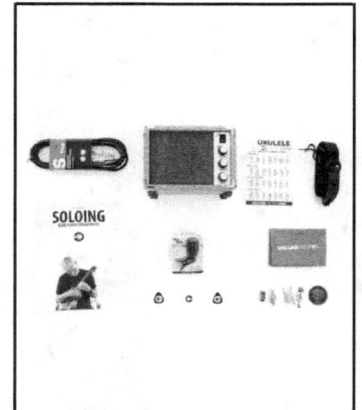

Accessories

UKELIKETHEPROS.COM
BLOG.UKELIKETHEPROS.COM
TERRYCARTERMUSICSTORE.COM
BUYSTRINGSONLINE.COM
A7MUSICSCHOOL.COM
AXLERBRAND.COM

@ukelikethepros

INTERESTED IN GUITAR CONTENT?
ROCKLIKETHEPROS.COM

www.ingramcontent.com/pod-product-compliance
Lightning Source LLC
LaVergne TN
LVHW080041090426
835510LV00041B/1927